Buddhism

By F. Otto Schrader

Copyright © 2021 Lamp of Trismegistus. All rights reserved. No part of this publication may be reproduced or transmitted in any form or by any means, electronic or mechanical, including photocopying, recording, or by any information storage and retrieval system, without permission in writing from Lamp of Trismegistus. Reviewers may quote brief passages.

ISBN: 978-1-63118-567-0

*Esoteric Classics:
Eastern Studies*

Other Books in this Series and Related Titles

Aurora of the Philosophers by Paracelsus (978-1-63118-507-6)

Clairvoyance and Psychic Abilities by A Besant &c (978-1-63118-403-1)

The Feminine Occult by various authors (978-1-63118-711-7)

Rosicrucian Rules, Secret Signs, Codes and Symbols by various (978-1-63118-488-8)

An Outline of Theosophy by C W Leadbeater (978-1-63118-452-9)

Paracelsus, the Four Elements and Their Spirits by M P Hall (978-1-63118-400-0)

Essays on Ancient Magic by Helena P Blavatsky (978-1-63118-535-9)

Essays on the Esoteric Tradition of Karma by A Besant &c (978-1-63118-426-0)

The Use of Evil by Annie Besant (978-1-63118-532-8)

The Alchemical Catechism of Paracelsus by Paracelsus (978-1-63118-513-7)

Alchemy in the Nineteenth Century by Helena P Blavatsky (978-1-63118-446-8)

Qabbalistic Teachings and the Tree of Life by M P Hall (978-1-63118-482-6)

The Historic, Mythic and Mystic Christ by Annie Besant (978–1–63118–533–5)

The Hidden Mysteries of Christianity by Annie Besant (978–1–63118–534–2)

History, Analysis and Secret Tradition of the Tarot by Hall &c (978-1-63118-445-1)

Crystal Vision Through Crystal Gazing by Frater Achad (978-1-63118-455-0)

The Golden Verses of Pythagoras: Five Translations (978-1-63118-479-6)

Arcane Formulas or Mental Alchemy by W W Atkinson (978-1-63118-459-8)

The Machinery of the Mind by Dion Fortune (978-1-63118-451-2)

The A E Waite Reader: A Selection of Occult Essays (978-1-63118-515-1)

The Leadbeater Reader: A Selection of Occult Essays (978-1-63118-483-3)

Audio versions are also available on Audible, Amazon and Apple

Other Books in this Series and Related Titles

Death by W W Westcott (978–1–63118–566–3)

The Religion of Theosophy by Bhagwan Das (978–1–63118–565–6)

The Spirit of Zoroastrianism by Henry S Olcott (978–1–63118–564–9)

The Brotherhood of Religions by Annie Besant (978–1–63118–563–2)

Fourth Book of Maccabees by Josephus (978-1-63118-562-5)

The Story of Ahikar by Ahiqar (978-1-63118-561-8)

Vision of the Spirit by C. Jinarajadasa (978-1-63118-560-1)

Occult Arts by William Q. Judge (978-1-63118-559-5)

Kali the Mother by Sister Nivedita (978-1-63118-558-8)

Love and Death by Sri Aurobindo (978–1–63118–557–1)

Times and Seasons Volume 1, Numbers 4-6 (978-1-63118-556-4)

The Book of John Whitmer by John Whitmer (978-1-63118-554-0)

Interesting Account of Several Remarkable Visions (978-1-63118-553-3)

The Evening and Morning Star Volume 1, Numbers 11 & 12 (978-1-63118-552-6)

Private Diary of Joseph Smith 1832-1834 (978-1-63118-546-5)

An Address to All Believers in Christ Elder David Whitmer (978-1-63118-545-8)

A Manuscript on Far West by Reed Peck (978-1-63118-544-1)

The Story of Mormonism by James E Talmage (978-1-63118-543-4)

The Philosophy of Mormonism by James E Talmage (978-1-63118-542-7)

The Angel of the Prairies or A Dream of the Future (978-1-63118-541-0)

The Book of Abraham: Mormon History by George Reynolds (978-1-63118-540-3)

Audio versions are also available on Audible, Amazon and Apple

Table of Contents

Introduction…7

Buddhism by F. Otto Schrader…9

INTRODUCTION

The word "esoteric" can be difficult to define. Esotericism in general can be seen less as a system of beliefs and more as a category, which encompasses numerous, different systems of beliefs. It's a bit of juxtaposition, since the word "esoteric" indicates something that few people know about, while the term itself broadly covers numerous philosophies, practices, areas of study and belief systems.

In a greater sense, Esotericism acts as a storehouse for secret knowledge, which is often considered ancient (by *tradition, if not by fact),* passed down from generation to generation, in private. At various times in history, simply possessing the knowledge of some of these subjects, was considered illegal and a jailable offence, if discovered. This usually included such general topics as Alchemy, Pharmacology, Qabalah, Hermeticism, Occultism, Ceremonial Magic, Astrology, Divination, Rosicrucianism and so on. Collectively, these areas of study were often referred to as the esoteric sciences.

Sometimes, the outer garment of a subject isn't esoteric, while what is hidden beneath it, is. As an example, Freemasonry isn't necessarily esoteric by nature (at *least not anymore),* but certain signs, passwords and handshakes given to the candidate during their initiation, are in fact, esoteric, in the sense that they are hidden from the general public.

Today, in the twenty-first century, such topics are readily available at bookstores across the country, and numerous mainsteam publishers offer beginners guides and coffee-table volumes on many of these subjects, intended for mass appeal. Books like *"The Secret"* have turned previously arcane topics into household knowledge. All that being the case, however, it isn't to say that there still aren't buried secrets to uncover, ancient wisdom being ignored and forgotten mysteries to be explored. In fact, it is often that we are only able to further our own studies by standing on the shoulders of these disappearing giants.

Lamp of Trismegistus is doing its part to help preserve humanity's esoteric history by making some of these classics available to those students who are seeking to unearth the knowledge of these ancient colossi.

So, be sure to check other titles from our *Esoteric Classics* series, as well as our *Occult Fiction, Theosophical Classics, Foundations of Freemasonry Series, Supernatural Fiction, Paranormal Research Series, Studies in Buddhism* and our *Christian Apocrypha Series*. You can also download the audio versions of most of these titles from Amazon, Apple or Audible, for learning on the go.

BUDDHISM

By Dr. F. Otto Schrader

Most visitors to India who come to understand to what an extent the religious life of the country is governed by the Brahmins, descendants of the ancient sacerdotal caste, are likely to take it as a matter of course that all religions of Hindu origin have been founded by members of that caste. This, however, is a complete error. Many, if not most, of the religious systems of ancient India have been founded by members of the Kshatriya or warrior caste, and only their later elaboration is, as a rule, due to the Brahmins.

Among the ancient Indian religions founded by noblemen and more or less opposed to the Brahmanic orthodoxy, at least originally, there are three which deserve particular attention, because they have in common one remarkable feature not to be found in any other of the existing religions of the world.

These three religions are: that of the Bhagavatas, that of the Jainas, and that of the Buddhists; and the peculiar feature they have in common is the belief in periodical appearances of Saviors appearing successively, within fixed periods, in order to start afresh or to restore to its purity the same religious system which all of their predecessors have preached.

The ancient religion of the Bhagavatas, now known as Vaishnavism, teaches that God, *i.e.,* Vishnu, incarnates at certain times of religious decadence in the body of some terrestrial being, animal or man, such an incarnation being called an Avatara or "Descent". The most famous is the Krishna Avatara, and the next to come is the Kalki Avatara.

The Jainas believe that in the cycle of time in which we are living (*the length of which is expressed by a number covering about two millions of ciphers*), twenty-four Saviors, called Jainas (*Conquerors*) or Tirthankaras (*Pathmakers*), have appeared successively. The last of these, called Mahavira, was a contemporary of the Buddha, and we know that his predecessor, Parshvantha, is also a historical person; a suspicion has quite recently arisen that even one or two more of these apparently invented personalities, although of course not the dates to which they are assigned, may prove to be historical.

Buddhism also has the doctrine that, as there is an infinite number of world cycles, so there is an infinite number of Saviors of the world, these Saviors being called Buddhas or Awakened Ones, *i.e.,* men who have arisen from the sleep of existence. It is from these that Buddhism (*which ought to be Bauddhism*) has taken its name, just as Jainism (*or Jinism*) has from the Jinas, and Vaishnavism from Vishnu, the incarnating God. Out of the innumerable numbers of Buddhas some of the Buddhist texts mention by name only the last seven, others mention twenty-four (*of which, as of the twenty-four Jinas, there is a short biography*), and some even twenty-seven. There are some Kalpas or Kosmic periods in which no Buddha appears, the so-called "Empty Kalpas"; while in others there are from one to five Buddhas. We are now living in a Kalpa blessed with five Buddhas of whom the last, the Buddha Metteyya or Maitreya, is still expected to come 5,000 years after the historical Buddha, *i.e.*, about 2,500 years hence; or, according to another statement which does not quite agree with this, when the average life period of men, after having reached its lower limit of 10 years, will have again increased to 80,000 years. That the three Buddhas of this Kalpa prior to the historical one were, if not historical persons, yet actually worshiped as such during the first centuries after the rise of Buddhism, is proved by an inscription informing us that the great Buddhist Emperor Ashoka gave orders twice during his reign to elevate a certain artificial hill supposed to contain relics of the Buddha Konagamana. Konagamana according to the Buddhist scripture was the predecessor of Kassapa, and Kassapa was followed by the historical Buddha.

Buddhism is the most interesting and the most widely spread of the three religions mentioned, and it is an outline of this religion, which I propose to place before you this evening. I shall pass over with as few words as possible all that appears to me unessential for the understanding of this religion, in order to devote special attention to its philosophical basis, and particularly to the two points which have been most misunderstood both in India and in the West, the doctrine of the soul and that of Nirvana.

The claim of Buddhism to be studied in preference to the other Indian Religions lies in the fact, that, apart from its doctrines, Buddhism alone of all Indian religions has become a world-religion. The Brahmanic community is closed to all foreigners, and so is that of the Jains; no foreigner, however intense may be his devotion for Vishnu or Shiva or the Jinas, can ever become a member of the communities concerned, except by a new birth; but the door of Buddhism is open, now as ever, to people of any nationality, and it is surely a significant fact that increasing numbers of Europeans and Americans are actually joining the Buddhist community, some of them even entering the monastic order. I do not know whether the current statement that the Buddhist community counts at present 510 millions of souls is quite correct, for the ciphers obtainable from China are very doubtful; but this much is certain, that it far outnumbers any other religious community in the world, not excluding Christianity all of whose sects together reach only the number of 330 million souls. It is also certain that Buddhism alone of the three great world-religions has reached its success without ever staining the memory of its Founder with bloodshed.

Buddhism was founded in the sixth century before the Christ by Prince Siddhartha of the Shakya family. The Shakyas were the rulers of a small kingdom with hardly more than a million inhabitants, occupying the slopes of the Nepalese Himalaya about the region of the modern town of Gorakhpur, 100 miles approximately to the north-west of Benares. Though recognizing as their supreme ruler the King of Koshala, they were essentially independent; and they are described as a haughty clan tracing back their lineage to the ancient King Ikshvaku, famous in Indian legend. Their capital was Kapilavastu. The neighboring kingdoms included, besides

Koshala, the Empire of Magadha whose capital was Rajagriha, the Kingdom of the Vatsas, that of the Avantis, and the Confederation of the Vrijjis comprising eight states one of the latter being the Republic of the Licchavi, of Vaishali.

There is every reason to believe that the condition of Northern India at that time was a prosperous one, and not at all the picture of misery which writers on Buddhism used to construct in order to account for the appearance of that religion. It is also quite wrong to suppose that Buddhism appeared as something altogether unique and unheard of, like the religion of Mohammed in Arabia for example. The time of the Buddha was saturated with religious ideas of every description, new systems springing up and disappearing like mushrooms after the rain. The "Discourse of the Philosophical Net" (Brahmajala-Sutta) in which the Buddha declares that he has caught all the speculations of his time, mentions 62 philosophical standpoints; while the Scripture of the Jains brings the number of the *Darshanas* even up to 363. We are also now in a position to clearly recognize the nature of the rain, which had caused such a luxuriant growth; it was the feeling of intellectual freedom after a period of sacerdotal rule, which had seized the Indian mind. Among the six famous teachers mentioned so often in the *Nikayas* as the principal rivals of the Buddha, there is not one representative of the Vedic doctrines. Such being the conditions of the country, it is surely not very strange that even the crown-prince of a little kingdom should have felt the call to renounce his comfort in order to take part in the feverish search after Truth.

Tradition reports that King Shuddhodana, the father of Siddhartha, received a prophecy after the birth of the latter telling him that his son would renounce the world to become a great saint; and that, wishing to prevent the prophecy from coming true, he did everything in his power to make the world pleasant for him. He seemed to succeed for a while; but in his twenty-ninth year the young man had a series of visions; first of a man bent down by old age, then of a leper, then of a corpse, and finally of an ascetic, radiant with serenity. This became the turning point of his life; as he tells us himself in the *Majjhima-Nikaya,* he had the hairs of his head and beard shaved, put on the yellow robe of the wandering ascetic, and, in spite of the lamentations and tears of his parents, "went out from home into homelessness".

The problem the prince had before him was how to get rid of old age, disease, and death, which is tantamount, from the Hindu standpoint, to the question as to how to be liberated from the necessity of being born again and again. Not a metaphysical but a practical problem. Not actually the question "What is Truth?" but the question, "How to attain Perfection?" The Indian philosopher, fundamentally different in this respect from his western colleague, does not and never did want to discover Truth for the sake of Truth, that is to say merely in order to *know;* but he wanted it solely as a means to liberation. There were many at the time of Buddha, as indeed also previously, who pretended to have solved the problem of Liberation, and all of these solutions apparently belonged to one of three classes: firstly there was that of the orthodox or Vaidikas, who insisted faith in the Vedas and sacrifice was the one path to be followed; secondly there was the belief as old as the Vedas that asceticism, understood as a victory of the mind over the body, was the safest way to perfection; and lastly there was that of the philosophers who asserted that knowledge, *i.e.*, the perfect comprehension of the special philosophical system they severally proclaimed, with or without a certain practice of concentration called Yoga, was essential for the attainment of the highest goal.

The first of these three paths had ceased to be fashionable at the time in which we are interested, or at least in those regions of Northern India with which we are concerned; so the Prince when starting upon his search after truth vacillated between the other two, and actually tried both of them, one after the other, first philosophy and then asceticism. He became successively the disciple of two famous philosophers, living as recluses somewhere in or near the Nepalese Himalaya, named Alara Kalama and Uddaka Ramaputta, both of whom taught a variety of the philosophy known as Samkhya-Yoga from the great epic *Mahabharata*. He succeeded in mastering so completely these two systems that Alara asked him to become his associate, while Uddaka was even prepared to make him the leader of his school. Neither system, however, satisfied our Prince, because in his opinion the liberation taught was incomplete in both cases: the so-called liberated soul was not actually liberated from the limitations of individuality and was deemed to return to worldly existence, although only after an enormous period of rest.

He then turned to asceticism, and, knowing that patience was essential here, practiced many varieties of it for six long years. Towards the end of this period he lived at Uruvela, near Buddhagaya, in the company of five other ascetics, who had recognized his greatness, and had resolved to wait until "the ascetic Gotama" as he was called (*after the branch of the family of the Shakyas to which he belonged*) would have reached enlightenment. But they waited in vain; for, after having reduced his body to almost a skeleton (*there is a beautiful sculpture in the Calcutta Museum showing him in this state*) he fell down one day on the floor unconscious, and he was believed to be dead. He recovered, however, and then the bitter knowledge dawned upon him that he had been on the wrong path for so many years. "*Whatever hard austerities there are in the world,*" so he is reported to have said to himself, "*all those austerities I have experienced. And I have not reached that incomparable highest peace. Surely, this is not the right way to Liberation.*" So he began again to take regular food, and his companions, believing that he had fallen from the ideal, abandoned him and went to Benares. He then sat down under a fig-tree (*which became famous afterward as the Bodhi Tree or Tree of Enlightenment*) and began to reflect deeply. He remembered how once in the days of his boyhood, while he was sitting under a tree in the garden of the palace, he attained involuntarily a certain mental state which gave him supreme satisfaction; and suddenly he knew that it was through the Dhyanas (*Jhanas*) or stages of mystical meditation, which he had already practiced under his two Samkhya Yoga teachers, that he would reach enlightenment; so he took to the Dhyanas again, and, after having reached the fourth and highest of them, experienced at last what he had sought for so long: the *Mahabodhi* or Great Enlightenment.

The Great Enlightenment is said to have taken place during the three parts of that same night in the following way: in the first place the Prince was able to trace back his former existences, one by one up to a very remote past. In the second part he obtained an insight into the working of the law of Karman, or Retribution, by seeing the beings ascending to higher births and descending to lower ones in strict accordance with their deeds. In the third part the great doctrine of all the Buddhas was revealed to him, namely, that individual existence, including the highest one we can conceive of, is essentially suffering; that the desire for such existence is the only cause of it; that consequently the complete abandonment of such desire is Liberation; and that the efficacious means conducing to favorable births and finally to Liberation is the "Noble Eightfold Path," consisting of Right Views, Right Aims, Right Words, Right Behavior, Right Mode of Livelihood, Right Exertion, Right Mindfulness, Right Meditation and Tranquility. What all this means we shall see later on; here it suffices to state the two points in which the doctrine of the Buddha was believed by himself to differ essentially from those of his teachers, and of most or perhaps all religious teachers before him. These are: the knowledge that without the complete abandonment of any clinging to individual existence there can be no question of Liberation, and the discovery that morality is indispensable for religious progress.

The great enlightenment of Prince Siddhartha had the immediate effect of completely extinguishing all his passions; that is to say, in that blessed night he attained Nirvana, which means nothing else than "extinguishing," and consequently Liberation. The force driving to rebirth, the Thirst (tanha, *trishna*) as the Buddhists call it, had ceased to exist for him in this so called *Samditthika Nibbana* or "Extinction during life," and it was certain, therefore, that the remainder, namely, his body and mind *without* Thirst, would also cease to exist in the *Parinirvana* or "Complete Extinction" at the time of his death. After the night under the Bodhi tree the Buddha, as the Prince rightly called himself from that time, hesitated about proclaiming his knowledge, because the doctrine of Nirvana and that of the concatenation of causes (*Pratityasamutpada*) were sure to be misunderstood. But his intense love and compassion for suffering humanity at last conquered his doubt, and he made up his mind to bring the good news first to his two teachers, Alara and Uddaka, for whom he had a loving memory. He learnt, however, that both of them had died a very short time previously, so he started for Benares in order to meet and instruct the five ascetics who had been his companions. On the way there two merchants, Tapussa and Bhallika, offered him food and became his first lay disciples. The five ascetics at first refused to acknowledge him as a Buddha, but after he had delivered to them his first sermon (*the so-called Sermon of Benares*) on the two extremes to be avoided, namely, worldliness and asceticism, and on the four Noble Truths concerning Suffering and Liberation, they joined him as personal disciples. The next lay convert was a rich young man called Yashas, whose example was followed by most of his relatives and friends; and after this the community grew so rapidly that the Buddha's audience at his second sermon consisted of a thousand monks. This second sermon, which was, like the first, a private lecture to the monks, is called the Buddhist "Sermon on the Mount," because it was delivered on the hill Gayashirsha. A better name, referring to its contents, is "The Sermon on Fire," everything existing, especially the passions, being compared with flames in it. Buddha then went to Rajagriha, the capital of King Bimbisara who became one of his sincerest admirers and protectors and presented the Order with a large park, the Veluvana. Here also were won by the Buddha those two disciples who were to play the most important roles after himself in the community, Shariputra and the Maudgazayana.

On a second visit to Rajagriha, four more important disciples joined the Buddha, namely, his cousins Ananada and Devadatta, and Anuruddha and Upali. Ananda is the Saint John of Buddhism, that disciple of whom the Lord was especially fond; in a poem said to be composed by himself he says: "I have served the Lord for twenty-five years, with love, with my heart, mouth, and hands, not abandoning him, like his shadow." Devadatta is the traitor of the Buddha, he undertook to murder the Lord, after the latter had declined to nominate him as his successor and place him at the head of the community. He failed however, but then he caused a schism by persuading a number of monks to lead, under his guidance, a more ascetic life than the one prescribed by the Buddha, by living only in forests, never begging in villages, never accepting an invitation, strictly avoiding fish and meat, and so forth. This Order of Devadatta still existed in the seventh century A.D. as a Buddhist sect which did not recognize the historical Buddha, but only the preceding Buddhas.

When Buddha visited his native town Kapilavastu, he had a very cold reception, his relatives considering it as an offence to their noble family that he went about as a beggar. Soon, however, they bowed to his greatness, and his son Rahula entered the Order. Not long afterwards Shuddhodana, the father of the Buddha, died, and his wife Mahaprajapati, the Buddha's stepmother, demanded to be admitted into the Order. Thrice the Buddha declined her entreaty. At last, on the request of Ananda, he consented to the establishment of an Order for nuns, but not without adding the prophecy that now the pure doctrine would exist only for 500 instead of 1,000 years. About three months before the death of the Buddha two events are reported to have happened which show how great had become the esteem in which he was held, the second one being characteristic of him also in another way: he succeeded in preventing a war between King Ajatashatru and Vrijjis of Vaishali, and he accepted an invitation to dinner from the "town-beauty" of Vaishali, the courtesan Amrapali; hearing of her success some young Licchavi nobleman tried in vain to purchase that honor from her for 100,000 gold coins. Later on Amrapali became a nun, like some others of her profession, and the stanzas ascribed to her in the *Therigatha* belong to the finest of that collection.

Of the end of the Master we have a touching report written in beautiful old Pali prose, the *Mahaparinibbana Sutta*. We learn from it that the Buddha when he was eighty years old, after having recovered from a severe illness in Beluva near Vaishali where he had passed the rainy season, started for Kushinagara, the capital of the Mallas, and on the way became ill again owing to a meal of mushrooms (*or if the usual interpretation of the word is correct, of pork*) offered to him by the smith, Chunda, in the village, Pava. In a little grove under two blossoming Sal trees, he had his last couch prepared by Ananda. He instructed Ananda to tell Chunda that he would have a very great reward for the meal the latter had given him; and he discussed with him details about his funeral and about other things concerning the Order. When at last Ananda could not restrain his grief, going aside and weeping bitterly, the Buddha called him back and comforted him with great and kind words. Then a Brahmin philosopher, Subhadra, arrived in order to ask the Buddha some questions, and he became his last convert. When the Master felt his end approaching he turned to the monks and spoke those words which were the last to fall from his lips: *Hanta dani, bhikkhave amantayami vo; vayadhamma sankhara appamadena sampadadetha!* "Now then, ye monks, I am speaking to you: all thing are subject to decay; be on your guard and work out your perfection!" He then entered the Dhyanas, just as he had done on the eve of his Enlightenment, and passed away. His body was cremated with royal honors by the Mallas in whose country his death had occurred, and his ashes were distributed by the Brahmin Drona among the several Princes who were present. The portion that fell to the share of the Shakyas was discovered 16 years ago, an inscription on the urn containing it leaving no doubt about its genuineness.

The unique success of the Buddha may be ascribed to four causes: The first cause lay in the favorable social condition of his time which was one of transition, a religious interregnum, as it were, between the Vedic period of childlike belief and the long period of intellectual slavery which has not ended even yet. To understand this, we need only imagine a nobleman like the Buddha appearing now, say in the Tamil country, and trying to convert the Brahmins of Chidambaram or the quarrelling Vaishnavas of Conjeevaram. His success would hardly be greater than that of the Brahma Samaj. For not only were religious prejudices, generally speaking, much less accentuated than they are now, but also the rigorous caste rules now obtaining did not yet exist in the Buddha's time, as is proved, apart from other things, by the occasional mention in the Buddhist texts of people changing their professions. The second cause of the Buddha's success was, of course, the excellence of his doctrine, its broadness, its suitability for the needs of the India of his time. The third cause was the eminently practical way in which the doctrine was preached by directly appealing to the people through similes, and by strictly avoiding metaphysical discussions. And last, not least, we have to take into account the overwhelming greatness of the personality of the Buddha, of which there are many testimonials of an historical character in the *Pitakas, e.g.,* the frequent reports of a complot of Brahmins who came to refute publicly the Buddha in a certain premeditated way but grew dumb as soon as they saw him; or the complaint of a king about the noisiness of his ministers when he addressed them, while a leaf might be heard falling to the ground even in an assembly of thousands of people as soon as the Buddha opened his mouth.

So much about the life of the Buddha, his time and his personality. We will now try to understand his principal doctrines. Of these the most important one, both from the metaphysical and the ethical points of view, and the one, which has been most misunderstood, is the doctrine of the *anatta* (anatman) or Not-Self. It came to be interpreted in quite different manners even among the Buddhists themselves, and a long discussion on the subject arose between them and the Vedanta philosophers, which ended only a few centuries ago when practically all Buddhists had left India. In Europe it was at one time concluded from this doctrine that Nirvana meant absolute annihilation, and that the Buddha taught metempsychosis without a *psyche, i.e.,* that he taught reincarnation but denied that there was a reincarnating soul.

The source of all errors on the Buddha's doctrines of the Not-Self is the ambiguity of two words.

The Sanskrit word *atman* or Self, Pali *atta,* must have meant originally the individual soul conceived of as "breath," as is shown by the undeniable connection of the word *atman* with the German word for breath, namely *atem,* and also by the Greek word *pneuma* meaning both breath and spirit. But in the Vedic time preceding the rise of Buddhism it came to be used in two other senses by descending, as it were to a lower, and on the other hand rising to a higher plane, namely (1) in the sense of "body," and (2) in the sense of the "Absolute," *i.e.,* God as the impersonal ground of the world, which is our Self in so far as it is in us as the ever-present ultimate root of our existence. Thus it came about that the immutability of the Highest Self, or the Timeless Self as we may call it, was erroneously transferred to the individual soul, so that the latter came to mean something permanent, a substance, which is philosophically an absurdity because we cannot really conceive of a thing existing in time but not subject to change. It is this absurdity to which, more than a thousand years after the Buddha, even the great philosopher Shankaracharya fell a victim in explaining memory by means of the permanence of the Self; and it is this absurdity and nothing else which the Buddha meant to combat in his innumerable warnings never to consider as a "Self" anything existing in the world. Why he laid so much stress on it we shall understand later on, when we come to his ethics; but we must here explain why the Highest Self of Brahmanism the Param Brahma or Paramatma, was not referred to by him as the true Self, but on the contrary was also considered as Not-Self. The reason is: that just as attributes of the Timeless Self had been erroneously transferred to the individual Self, so the former has been mixed up with the latter, by attributing to it consciousness and other features which it is in reality impossible to imagine as separated from time, *i.e.*, the world. The Highest Brahman, therefore, was to the Buddha, although not a non-entity, yet not essentially different from the Lower Brahman, the Ruler of a solar system, with whom indeed it appears to have become amalgamated, as a rule, in the Brahmanism of the Buddha's time. Still, it might be asked, why did not the Buddha *correct* the Brahmanic conception of the Absolute? To this the answer is that he did correct it, but by silence. For three reasons he refrained from speaking on this point: firstly, because it was a principle with him to strictly avoid philosophical discussions - he declined to be a philosopher, nay, warned against philosophy, and made a sharp difference between philosophical knowledge and *panna prajna, i.e.,* spiritual insight obtainable by his doctrine; secondly, he knew from the Brahmanic systems that it was dangerous to speak about the Absolute; and thirdly, he knew that in his case it was superfluous, because his doctrine was the safest way to realize that which can never be described but merely stated as "a negative border-idea." (ein *negativer Grenzbegriff),* to use an expression of the most renowned German philosopher.

The other word which is responsible for the misinterpretation of the theory of the Not-Self, and more particularly for the strange assertion that the Buddha taught metempsychosis without a *psyche,* is the word *vijnana,* Pali *vijnnana,* which means spirit or consciousness. The Buddha excluded the word "Self" from the terminology of his system on account of the philosophical error which had become associated with it: his declaration that there is nowhere a Self in the world means simply and solely that there exists no permanent individuality. But Professor Rhys Davids and other writers on Buddhism understood it to mean that there is no soul at all, and they believed that this interpretation was corroborated by the Buddha's doctrine of the Skandhas, Pali *Khandhas,* Skandha means "stem," also "complex," "department," or "section." The word was used by the Buddha to designate the five classes of phenomena which he found to be expressed in every human being, namely, (1) the body, (2) the feelings (pleasure and pain), (3) the sensations, (4) the samskaras, or latent impressions, including most of what we call character, and (5) the *vijnana* or thought. This classification becomes less strange if we remember that for the Indian there is not that sharp dividing line between matter and consciousness which is so conspicuous in European philosophy, consciousness having always been regarded by him as a sort of fine matter. Now the teaching is, that at the time of death these five Skandhas disintegrate in order to be replaced by a new set of Skandhas at the time of rebirth, which new set is in every respect the exact continuation of the old one. It would seem, then, that there is no connecting link between the old and the new set; that is to say, that there is missing here the *jivatma* or individual soul of Brahmanism, which runs like a thread through the innumerable existences of each individual. However, the *jivatma* is *not* missing in Buddhism, although it is never called there by that word because the word *atman* or Self, as we have seen, was debarred. The word used for it is *vijnana;* but this *vijnana* is not the same as the Skandha mentioned above, for it is the "element" called consciousness, the *vijnana-dhatu*. This is, according to Buddhism, a sixth element to be added to earth, water, fire, wind and ether; and while the human body, *i.e.,* the first or material Skandha, is a *compound* of these five other elements, the *vijnana,* or soul-element, as we may now call it, is a *unit* of which the four other Skandhas are mere manifestations during life. What really happens, then, at the time of death is this: the four "Consciousness-Skandhas" (cetasika *khandha)* as they are called become latent in the unit underlying them, and that unit, called in this condition, in which it has no manifestations, the *patisandhi-vinnana,* or "rebirth-consciousness," transmigrates immediately or later to the particular being by which it is attracted in the act of conception. There are passages in the Buddhist Scriptures speaking of the "descent" of *vijnana* into the womb of the mother, which leave no doubt as to the correctness of our explanation, which moreover is sufficiently warranted by the very existence of the word *patisandhi-vinnana* "rebirth- consciousness", To be quite Buddhistic, however, we must add the remark that the soul-element is more permanent than the body only in that its flow, as it were, is not interrupted by death. In itself it is changing every moment, its vibrations being so rapid that in this regard the Buddha once called it less permanent than the body. This soul-unit, though outliving the death of innumerable bodies, at last has also its death: it comes to a sudden end in the death of the Liberated.

What then takes place at this final death, the Parinirvana? The older disciples of the Buddha knew that the subject belongs to the Avyakhatas or things, which have not been, and cannot be, explained - to the mysteries. But the younger ones, as well as laymen and strangers, often asked the Buddha this question, without ever obtaining a definite answer. Consequently it has been conjectured by Professor Rhys Davids and many others, that the Parinirvana has no positive side at all but signifies absolute annihilation, and that the Buddha preferred to be silent about it because he was afraid that the unveiled truth would be an obstacle to the spread of his doctrine. That argument sounds quite plausible, but it shares with the above-mentioned explanation of Not-Self as Not-Soul, the defect of being a judgment based on incomplete material. I have shown nine years ago, in an article on the "Problem *of Nirvana*" published in the *Journal of the Pali Text Society,* that the Parinirvana has undoubtedly a positive side. Nothing has been published since which would controvert my arguments; while, in this connection, a German scholar who agrees with me, has called attention to a scholastic saying which sounds as if it had been coined with special regard to our problem, though it author of course knew nothing of Buddhism, namely: *Nec taliter nec aliter sed totaliter aliter,* which means: "Neither in such a way nor in a different way, but in a totally different way", or when translated into Buddhist language, in the words of the *Sutta-Nipata* in a passage on the condition of the Liberated One after death: "To say of him: 'He exists,' that is not correct; nor is it correct to say: 'He does not exist'; where everything imaginable has ceased, there all possibilities of speech have also ceased." In another text we read that a monk was once cited before the Buddha and rebuked by him because he had conceived the heretical opinion that the Liberated One after death is completely annihilated. These and similar passages, if taken together, prove beyond a shadow of doubt that Parinirvana, though meaning indeed "the total decomposition of the mental and the physical individuality," means at the same time "the passing of conditioned being into unconditioned being".

We must now consider the doctrine of *karman,* which I have previously mentioned without going into details. The doctrine of *karman,* Pali *kamma* teaches that every *karman,* or "work" which we do with either our body or our speech or our mind, *i.e.,* every action, every word and every thought of ours, so far as they are not ethically indifferent (neither good nor bad), leaves in the mind a certain impression - or, as Professor Pischel humorously calls it, a bacillus - which in the near or remote future inevitably develops into some pleasant or painful condition or event in our life, accordingly as the causative deed was a good one or a bad one. As has often been pointed out, the doctrine of Karman is, as it were, an exact elaboration of the Biblical saying: "Whatsoever a man soweth, that shall he also reap." There is, however, a remarkable difference between the Brahmanical and the Buddhistic conception of Karman: according to the former the *samskara* or disposition created by *karman,* I mean the bacillus referred to, being in itself unconscious, requires a conscious superintendent who takes care that the right effect of a deed comes out at the right time, and this post of a superintendent of Karman is given in the Brahmanic religions to the God Brahma (*who, by the way, would seem to have nothing to do otherwise*), or to Vishnu, or to Shiva; whereas Buddhism rejects the possibility of any such supervision, for the simple reason that the superintendents show by their being engaged in works that they are not liberated, and consequently require to be superintended themselves. Buddhism therefore holds that Karman works automatically, and that there is not, as the Brahmins believe, a possibility of its being altered by the grace of a God or suppressed by asceticism. Even the Liberated One - who is rid of his Karman according to Brahmanism - is in Buddhism still subjected to the consequences of his former deeds until his Parinirvana. Another difference between Brahmanism and Buddhism as regards Karman, is that Buddhism, at least the Buddhism of Ceylon and Further India (*which on the whole represents the oldest stage of Buddhism known to us*) denies that *everything* is the effect of former deeds, the deeds themselves for example being not such effects but new beginnings as it were. This is why the Buddhist belief in Karman is nowhere found to produce that paralyzing effect which is so often observed in Brahmanic India, where Karman is to many really not much more than fate.

Karman is particularly active at the time of birth; for the new birth is entirely determined by the sum of Samskaras present at that time. If the balance had been favorable the individual would have risen to some heavenly world, if unfavorable it would have sunk down to hell or to an animal womb or to the realm of *Pretas* or ghosts; but in both cases there is a return to human existence when the good or bad Karman is exhausted. The *Milindapanha* speaks of the increasing feeling of sadness, which a god experiences when he comes into the last period of his long life. There is one class of gods which is exempt from return to the world of men, the gods of the four very highest heavens, the so called Arupa-Lokas or Spiritual Worlds *i.e.,* realms in which *rupa* or matter does not exist, but only consciousness in its sublimest forms. Those fortunate ones, therefore, who have worked out their salvation so far that only one more existence is necessary for them, are reborn either as men, or as gods in one of the Arupa-Lokas.

We must now turn our attention once more to the doctrine of the Not-Self, in order to understand the important part it plays in Buddhist morals. "Fight against passion" is the watchword of Buddhism, because only by the cessation of thirst or desire for existence can Liberation be reached. Any clinging to the "I" and to the "mine" must therefore be overcome. Now, according to the Buddha's doctrine, this egoistic clinging is based on an *error,* on the wrong belief that there is something permanent in me as an individual, some soul-substance, which remains the same in spite of all the changes I undergo. This error is detected by the doctrine of the Not-Self, showing that nothing whatever in the world is permanent even for the space of a moment; that everything and every being, if carefully analyzed, proves like the stem of the plantain-tree to consist of many leaves rolled one over the other without anything substantial in the center. There is a seeming unity and permanency in individual existence, but it is that of the flame consisting of innumerable particles, each of which changes every moment. Consequently he who has realized that neither his body, nor his feelings, nor his sensations, nor his volitions, nor his ideas, nor all of these together, nor any other thing or things constitute the supposed permanent Ego, the Self for which he used to toil in his worldly undertakings, that there is in fact no such Self at all, such a one is sure to get rid gradually of his egotism and to approach Liberation at a corresponding rate. The Buddha, therefore, recommended his monks, over and over again, to meditate on the body, or one of the mental Skandhas, or on some external object with the constant thought: "That is not mine; I am not that; that is not myself."

The doctrine of the Not-Self has produced the finest flower of Buddhist ethics, namely: its practice of love (maitri, Pali *metta).* To understand that nothing in particular is myself, is tantamount to recognizing *everything* as myself. A change of center takes place and the monk knowing Anatta begins to look at his fellow-creatures as part and parcel of himself. This is called the Liberation of the Mind (cetovimuki, Pali *cetovimutti*), of which the Buddha says in the *Itivuttaka:* "All the means in this life, ye monks, to acquire religious merit have not the value of a sixteenth part of love, the Liberation of the Mind."

And in another passage he declares that to produce Love in one's mind for a single moment is a more commendable deed that to distribute among the poor thrice a day a hundred pots of food. The monks are recommended to sit down in a lonely place and to send out thoughts of "immeasurable love" for all beings into the four quarters, one after the other, then to the zenith and to the nadir: they should endeavor to actually love all beings with the love of a mother who protects with her life her only child. If somebody is unkind to him, the monk has to permeate him with the spirit of love. Even if robbers torture him in the most cruel way, says the *Majjhima-Nikaya,* no bad words should escape his lips, but pity and love only should he feel towards them.

This Buddhist love is different from the Christian love in that it does not admit of any passion, or any fanaticism whatever, any victory of feeling over reason. Being passionless benevolence, it is of course also quite different from *Bhakti* or love for God, as this implies a clinging. I may notice here, by the way, that Buddhism has no Personal God like the one of Brahmanism and Christianity, and is therefore in this sense really atheistic.

The spirit of love so prominent in Buddhism shows itself also in the very first of the five precepts which every Buddhist, layman and monk, must promise to keep, the precept not to destroy life, about which the *Dhammika Sutta* says the following: "Let him not destroy or cause to be destroyed any life at all, or sanction the acts of those who do so. Let him refrain from even hurting any creature, both those that are strong and those that tremble in the world." The remaining four precepts are: not to steal, not to commit adultery, not to tell lies, not to indulge in intoxicating drinks.

Many more things might be said about the Buddhist moral code, but they refer to minor points only; suffice it to say that it has always been much admired, even by those who came to convert these Buddhist pagans and atheists. There are also a few philosophical doctrines, which I have not discussed, and I have not been able to say anything about the constitution of the Order or about the history of Buddhism, which is exceedingly interesting. But if I have succeeded in convincing you that the Buddhist religion is very much more than a mere relic of the past, that it is indeed likely to have a greater future than most of the existing religions, then perhaps you may endeavor to become acquainted with the works on Buddhism and with the many translations already available of parts of one of the grandest Scriptures of the world.

www.ingramcontent.com/pod-product-compliance
Lightning Source LLC
LaVergne TN
LVHW041503070426
835507LV00009B/796